It's Fun to Cook!

By Jennifer Fellows

Pictures by Ann Rees

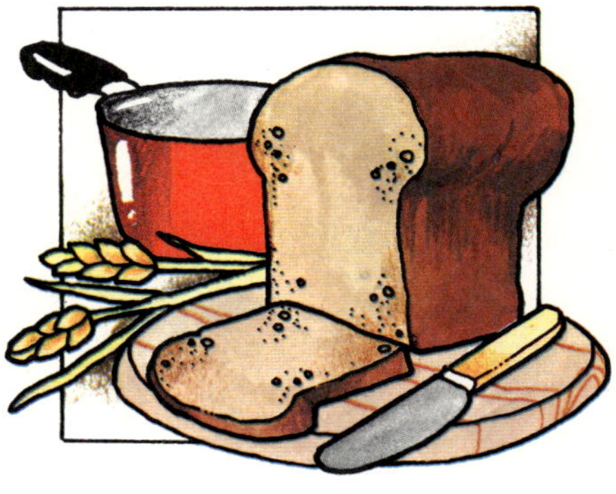

Gareth Stevens Publishing
Milwaukee

BRIGHT IDEA BOOKS:

First Words!
Picture Dictionary!
Opposites!
Sounds!

The Four Seasons!
Pets and Animal Friends!
The Age of Dinosaurs!
Baby Animals!

Doctor Wotsit's Zoo!
My Day at School!
Old Farm, New Farm!
Your Favorite Fairy Tales!

Mouse Count!
Time!
Animal ABC!
Animal 1*2*3!

Homes Then and Now!
Other People, Other Homes!

Dressing Up!
It's Fun to Cook!
Make It with Odds and Ends!

Space Trip!
Getting Around!
On Wheels!

Library of Congress Cataloging-in-Publication Data

Fellows, Jennifer.
It's fun to cook!

(Bright idea books)
Bibliography: p.
Summary: An introduction for children, grades three and up, to basic cooking and meal-planning principles, presenting recipes and menus with "favorite ingredients."
1. Cookery — Juvenile literature. [1. Cookery] I. Rees, Ann, ill. II. Title.
TX652.5.F47 1986 641.5'123 85-30311
ISBN 1-55532-042-2
ISBN 1-55532-017-1 (lib. bdg.)

This North American edition first published in 1986 by

Gareth Stevens, Inc.
7221 West Green Tree Road Milwaukee, Wisconsin 53223, USA

Typeset by Ries Graphics ltd.
Series Editors: MaryLee Knowlton and Mark J. Sachner
Cover Design: Gary Moseley
Reading Consultant: Kathleen A. Brau

Contents

Using the Kitchen

A Note to Kids Who Cook:

Here are some basic safety rules for the kitchen that will help you avoid accidents:

- Always have an adult present when you use the stove top or oven.
- Have an adult turn on the stove top or oven.
- When you use the stove top, always turn pot handles to the inside to prevent pots from accidentally being knocked off the stove.
- Turn the stove off after removing pots or pans. Double check!
- Always use gloves or mitts to take hot dishes out of the oven.
- Always have an adult present when you use a sharp knife.

Cook's Equipment

Cook's Cupboard

These basic ingredients will be used in many of the recipes. Always read the recipe before you begin and make sure you have all the ingredients.

Cook's Code

Always flour the tabletop or board before rolling out on it so that dough will not stick.

Always heat the oven before you begin so it can warm up.

How to knead: When kneading pastry, put it onto a floured top and press it with your fingers. Continue to fold it inwards and over, pressing it each time, about six times.

A pinch of salt is as much salt as you can hold between your thumb and first finger.

Always clean surfaces before and after you have used them.

When you mix sugar and butter or margarine, the mixture will turn pale yellow when it is fully blended.

Always grease and flour pans before using them to prevent the food from sticking.

Cooking Without a Stove

In making these dishes, you will not need any heat. The ingredients in each recipe can be mixed together without being melted.

Cheese and Pineapple Spikes

Can of pineapple chunks
A piece of cheese
Cherries (maraschino or fresh)
1 large potato
Tin foil, toothpicks, knife, strainer, plates

1

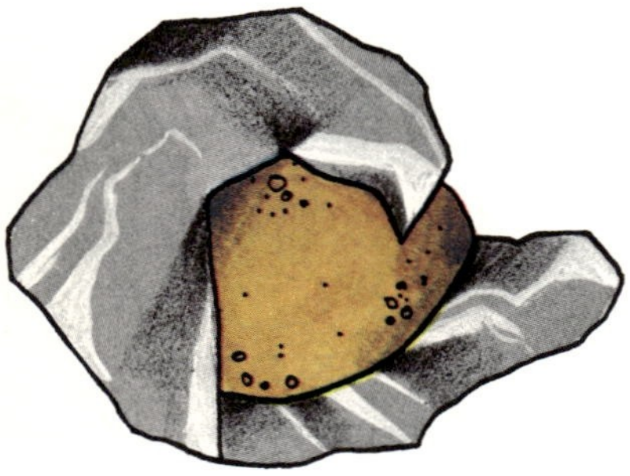

Wrap the potato in foil.

2

Ask a grown-up to open the can of pineapple. Using the strainer, pour out the juice.

3

Put the pineapple chunks onto a plate.

4

On the other plate, cut the cheese into small pieces.

5

Put chunks of cheese and pineapple on toothpicks and stick the toothpicks into the potato.

6

Continue until the cheese and pineapple are finished.

7

Add a few cherries for a more colorful effect.

Coconut Ice Shapes

1 small can of condensed milk
2¼ cups confectioners' sugar
¾ cup dried coconut
2 food colorings
Plate, 2 bowls,
strainer, wooden spoon, blunt knife

1

Have a grown-up open the can of milk and pour it into a bowl. Strain in the confectioners' sugar.

2

Mix the sugar and milk.

3

Add the coconut and stir. It should be very stiff.

4

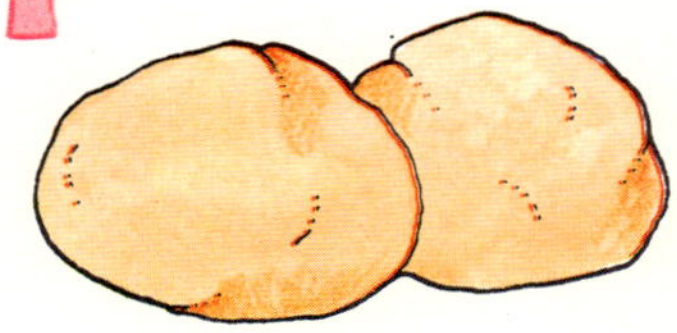

Divide the dough in half and put one piece in each bowl.

5

Add a little coloring to each piece and knead it in.

6

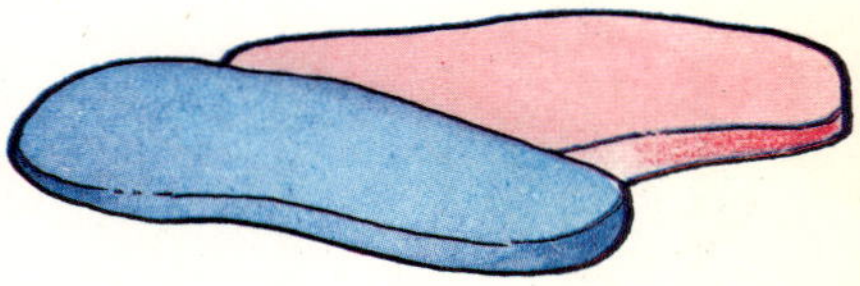

Press out each piece into a flat circle, about ¾ inch thick.

7

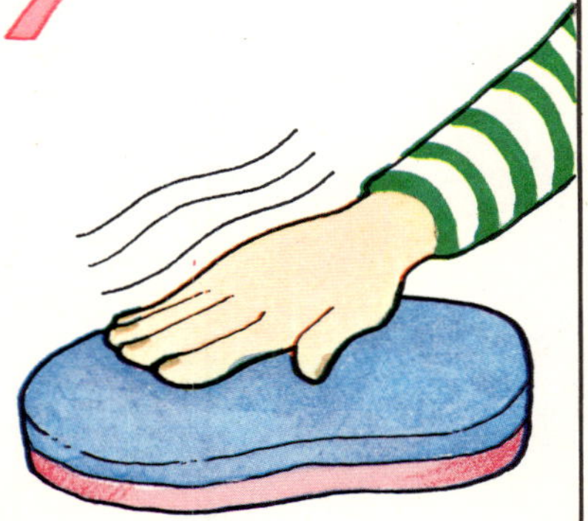

Press the circles together.

8

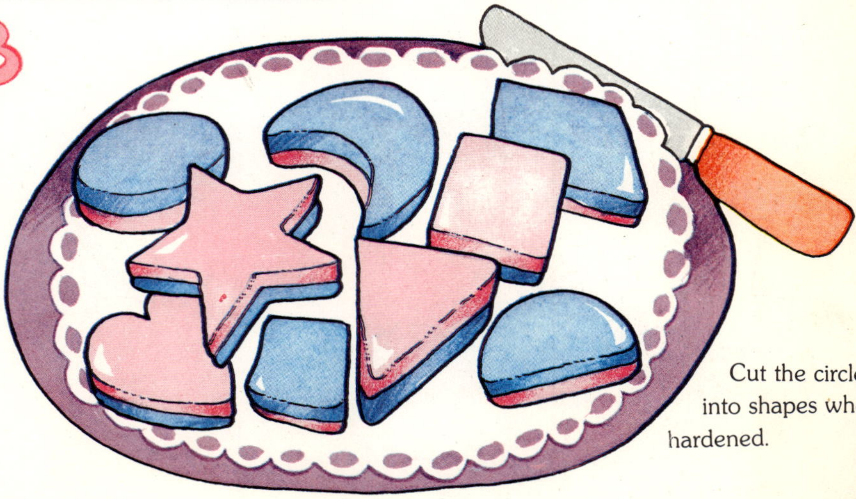

Cut the circles into shapes when hardened.

Salad Sandwich Boats

2 pieces of bread
Soft butter or margarine
2 slices of ham
2 pieces of cheese
4 lettuce leaves
1 tomato
1 apple
Cucumber/celery
8 radishes
2 toothpicks, knife, 2 plates

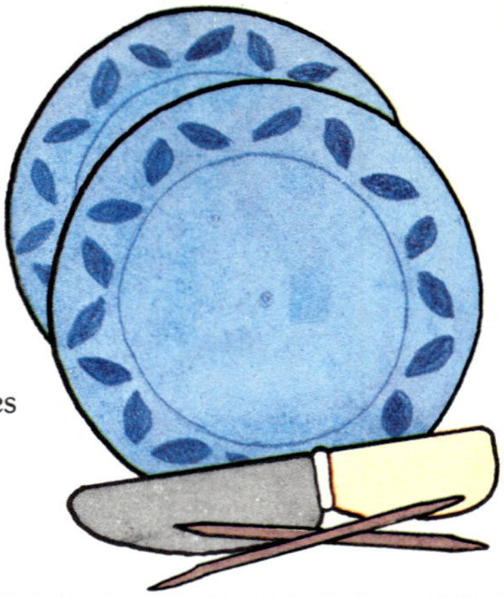

1

Butter the bread and put 1 slice on each plate.

2

Put 1 slice of ham on each slice of bread.

3

Decorate with a lettuce leaf.

4

Cut the tomato into pieces and divide the apple into small slices.

5

Put a piece of cheese in the middle of the sandwich boat and put pieces of apple and tomato around it.

6

Cut a piece of cucumber about 2½ inches long and divide it in half. To make oars, cut each half into four long strips.

7

Thread a lettuce leaf onto each toothpick and stand it in the cheese to make a sail.

8

Put the cucumber oars on either side of the plate.

9

Wash the radishes and put them at each oar as boatmen.

Peppermint Creams

3½ cups confectioners' sugar
1 egg white
½ lemon
Peppermint extract
Blunt knife, 2 bowls, cup and saucer, strainer, wooden spoon, rolling pin (or clean, empty bottle), 1 teaspoon

1

Strain the confectioners' sugar into a bowl.

2

Using a cup and saucer, divide the egg into white and yolk. (Ask a grown-up to help you!)

3

Put the egg white into the sugar and mix.

4

Knead the mixture well with your hands.

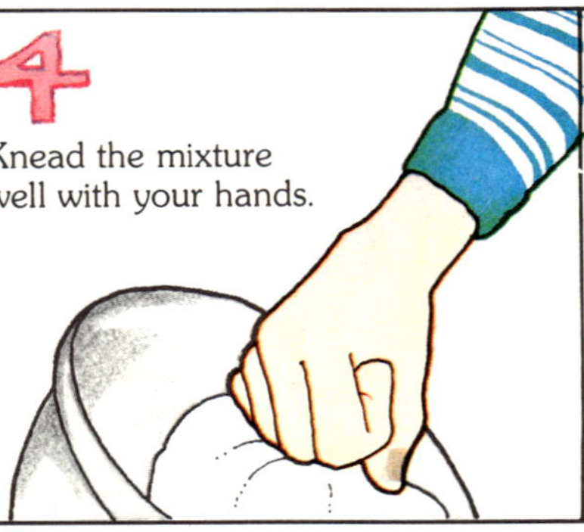

5

Add a little lemon juice and a few drops of peppermint extract. Knead again.

6

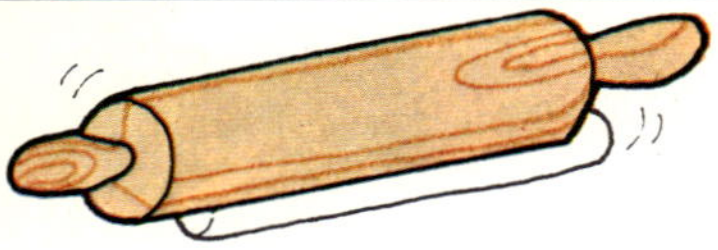

Pour a little sugar on the top of the table. Roll the mixture into a sausage.

7

Using a blunt knife, cut the sausage into small slices.

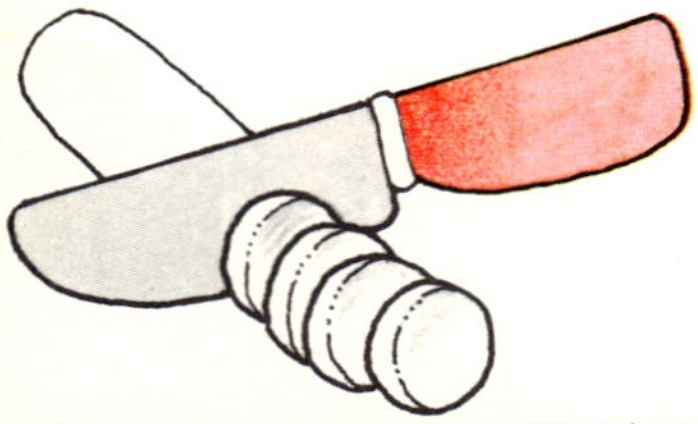

8

Arrange the slices on a plate and allow them to harden.

Marzipan Rolls

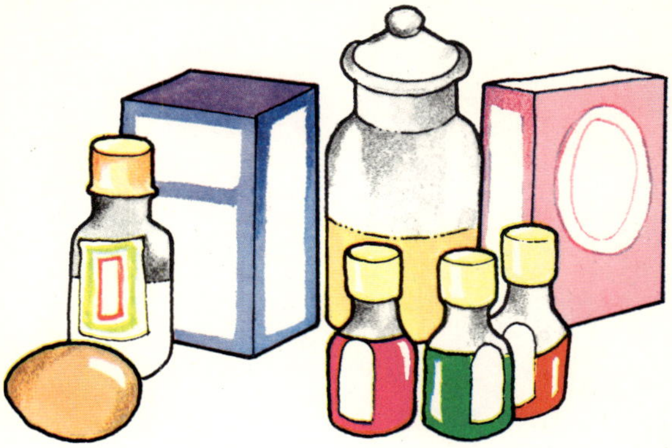

1 cup ground almonds
½ cup confectioners' sugar
½ cup sugar
Few drops of almond extract
Egg yolk to mix
3 food colorings
Bowl, fork, 2 cups

1

Put the ground almonds into a bowl and add confectioners' sugar, sugar, and a little almond extract.

2

Separate the egg yolk and white.

3

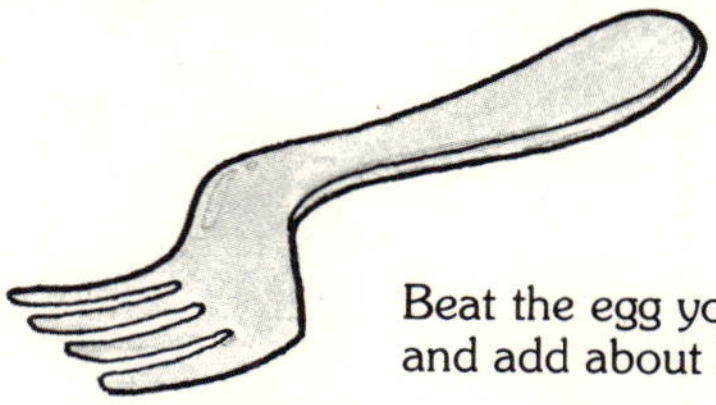

Beat the egg yolk a little with a fork and add about half to the bowl.

4

Mix the almonds, sugar, and egg yolk together with the fork. If it does not mix well, add a little more egg. If it is too wet, add a little more confectioners' sugar.

5

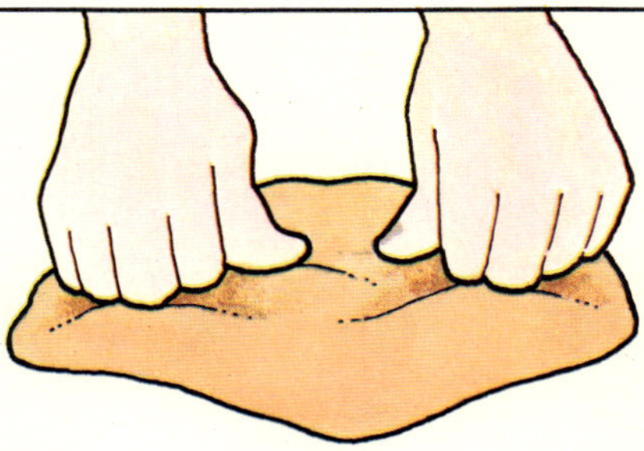

Put the mixture on a sugared table top and knead.

6

Divide the mixture into three parts. Put one part back into the bowl and add a little food coloring. Knead.

7

Do the same to the other two pieces and break each piece into small rolls. Allow the rolls to harden for about 1 hour.

Milk Shakes

2½ cups milk
Ice cream
Chocolate syrup,
fruit flavorings
or fruit
4 glasses
Pitcher
Whisk
Straws

If you don't have a blender:
Put 4 tablespoons of ice cream into a pitcher and pour on the milk. Add the flavoring and mix well. Pour the mixture into glasses.

If you have a blender:
Wash any fruit you like (apple, banana, raspberries), and cut it into small pieces. Put the milk, 4 tablespoons of ice cream, and fruit into the blender. Blend and pour the mixture into glasses.

For a special occasion, take out:

A piece of lemon
A glass
A saucer of sugar

Frost the glasses first. Then rub the lemon around the rim of the glass and dip the rim into the sugar.

Cooking on Top of the Stove or Under the Broiler

Whenever you see this sign ● it means that a grown-up should turn on the broiler or stove top.

When something cooks on top of the stove, the heat is rising through the ingredients. Stir the mixture constantly to spread the heat evenly.

When something cooks under the broiler, only the top of the food gets really hot.

When something is fried in a frying pan, the food must be turned over so that it cooks on both sides.

Grilled Ham and Cheese Sandwiches

2 slices of bread
2 slices of ham
1 tomato
2 slices of cheese
Knife
Plate

1

Toast the bread in a toaster or under the broiler.

2

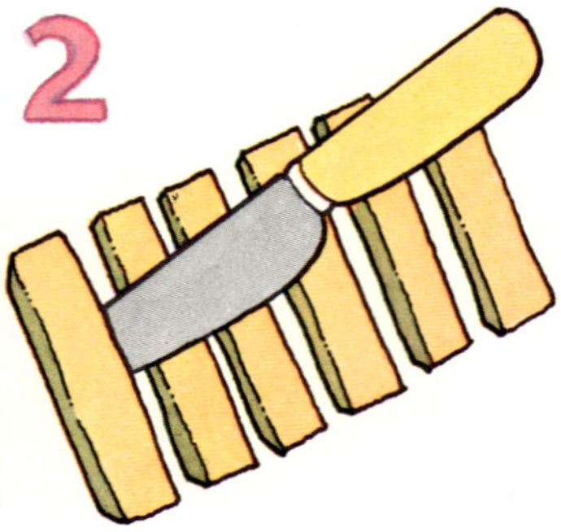

Cut the cheese slices into fingers.

3

Slice the tomato.

4

Put a slice of ham and some tomato on each piece of bread.

5

Put the cheese fingers on top of the tomato in a criss-cross pattern.

6

Put the sandwiches under the broiler and watch the cheese melt. When it begins to bubble, the sandwiches are ready.

They will be very hot.

French Toast

1 egg
Pinch of salt
2 tablespoons cold milk
2 slices of white bread
A little butter or margarine
Fork
Bowl
Frying pan
Spatula

1

Break the egg into the bowl and whisk with the fork.

2

Add the milk and salt.

3

Wet each piece of bread thoroughly in the egg mixture.

4

Put the butter into the frying pan over a medium flame or heat.

5

When the butter foams, put the bread into it and cook on each side.

6 Remove the bread when both sides are browned.

If you do not have a very large frying pan, you may have to cook one piece at a time.

Scotch Pancakes

2 cups all-purpose flour
¼ teaspoon salt
1 egg
1 tablespoon sugar
1¼ cups milk
A little shortening
Bowl
Wooden spoon
Large frying pan
Cup
Large spoon
Spatula, fork
Confectioners' sugar
Syrup

1

Put the flour and salt into the bowl and make a hollow in the middle.

2

Break the egg into the center of the flour and add a little milk. Begin to mix.

3

Go on adding the milk, a little at a time, stirring all the time.

4

Add sugar and mix again.

5

Heat the frying pan and melt the shortening so the pancakes will not stick.

6

Put a spoonful of the mixture into the pan. When bubbles rise, turn it over to brown the other side.

7

When the pancake is browned on the other side, remove it from pan. Continue with rest of mixture until it is all used up.

Serve the pancakes hot with butter and sprinkle with confectioners' sugar or syrup.

Potato Cakes

2½ cups cold mashed potatoes
1 cup flour
2½ tablespoons butter or margarine
Bowl
Fork
Frying pan
Spatula

1 Put the cold mashed potatoes, flour, and butter or margarine into the bowl and mix well with a fork.

2

Divide the mixture into about 12 little balls.

3 Flatten each ball until it is the size of a jam jar top and about ½ inch thick.

4 Fry the potato cakes in a frying pan, turning once.

Eat them with butter on top while they are still hot.

Cinnamon Toast

1 tablespoon ground cinnamon
3 tablespoons sugar
Sliced bread
Butter or margarine
Bowl
Spoon
Knife

1 Mix the sugar and cinnamon in the bowl.

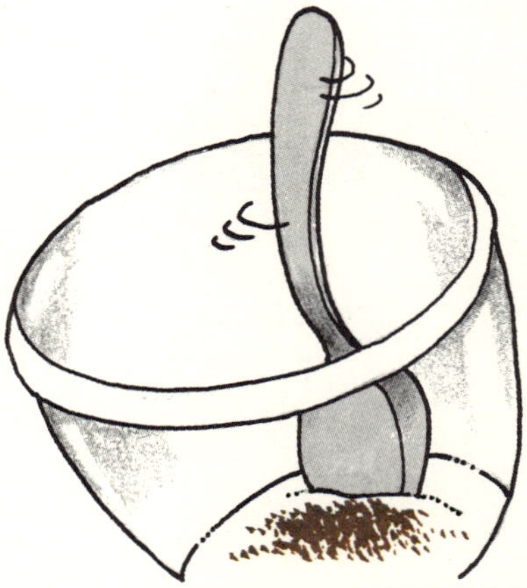

2 Toast the bread and butter it.

3 Sprinkle the toast with the cinnamon/sugar mixture.

4 Cut the toast into fingers or triangles and serve.

Sardine Fingers

Can of sardines
Black pepper
Vinegar
Bread
Butter or margarine
Bowl
Fork
Knife

1

Ask a grown-up to open the can of sardines for you.

2

Put the sardines into the bowl with a little black pepper and vinegar to taste, and mix with a fork.

3

Toast the bread and butter it.

4

Spread the toast with the sardine mixture and cut into fingers.

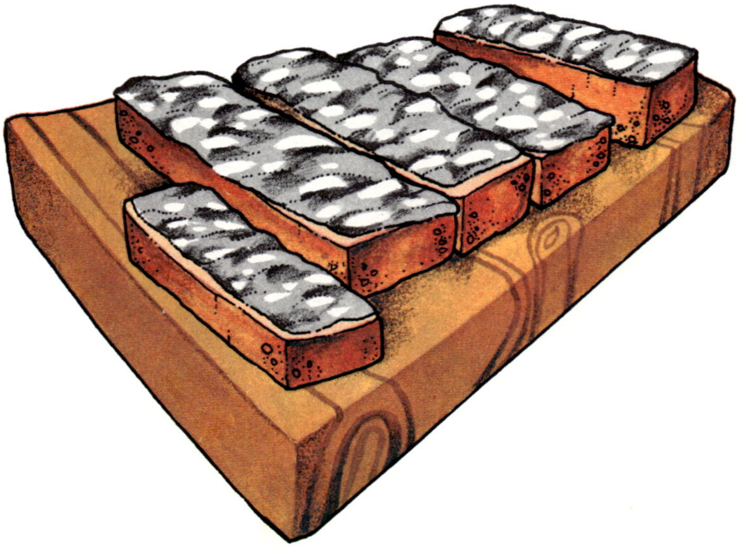

Chocolate Fudge

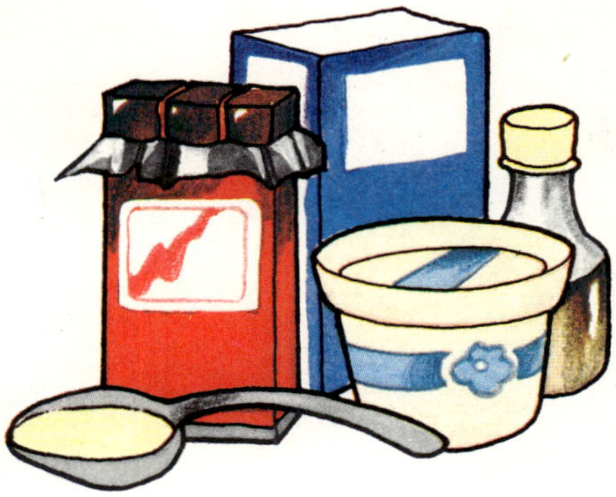

$\frac{1}{3}$ cup baking chocolate
2 tablespoons butter or margarine
$1\frac{1}{4}$ cups confectioners' sugar
1 tablespoon cream
4 drops vanilla extract
Saucepan
Bowl
Small cake pan
Wooden spoon

1 Break up the chocolate into the saucepan and add the butter.

2 Put the saucepan over a low heat until the chocolate melts. Then stir in the milk and vanilla extract.

3 Put the sugar into the bowl and pour on the chocolate mixture. Mix well.

4 Pour the mixture into the baking pan and let it cool.

5 When it is set, cut the fudge into little squares.

Crispy Chocolate Cupcakes

¼ cup butter or margarine
2 tablespoons butter or margarine
1 tablespoon maple syrup
1 cup cornflakes
¼ cup unsweetened cocoa
¼ cup confectioners' sugar
Wooden spoon
Saucepan
Paper cupcake holders
Plate or tray
Spoon

1 Put the butter and syrup into the saucepan and place the pan on a low heat.

2 When they have melted, remove the pan and mix the ingredients.

3 Add the sugar and the unsweetened cocoa and stir in well.

4 Add the cereal and mix in very gently until it is covered in the chocolaty mixture.

5 Put 16 paper cupcake holders on the tray. Put one spoonful of the mixture into each holder.

6 Let the cupcakes cool for about half an hour.

Baking in the Oven

Food bakes in the oven, where it is surrounded by heat. Heat rises, so the top of the oven is the warmest part and the bottom the coolest.

Always wear oven gloves when taking things out of the oven.

Remember, whenever you see this sign ● it means that a grown-up should turn on or light the oven.

Before you begin each recipe, check near the end of the recipe to see how hot the oven should be. Ask a grown-up to preheat the oven to that temperature.

Shortcrust Pastry

$1\frac{2}{3}$ cups all-purpose flour
$\frac{1}{2}$ cup butter or margarine
2 tablespoons cold water
Mixing bowl
Knife
Strainer
Plate

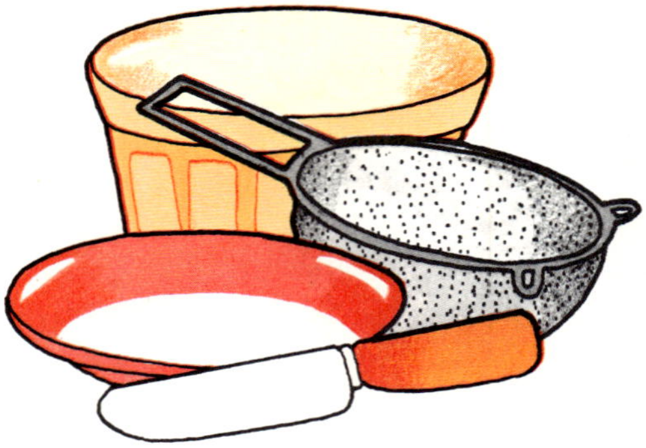

1 Strain the flour into a bowl.

2 Add the butter in small pieces.

3 Using the tips of your fingers, rub the flour and butter lightly together until it looks like breadcrumbs.

4

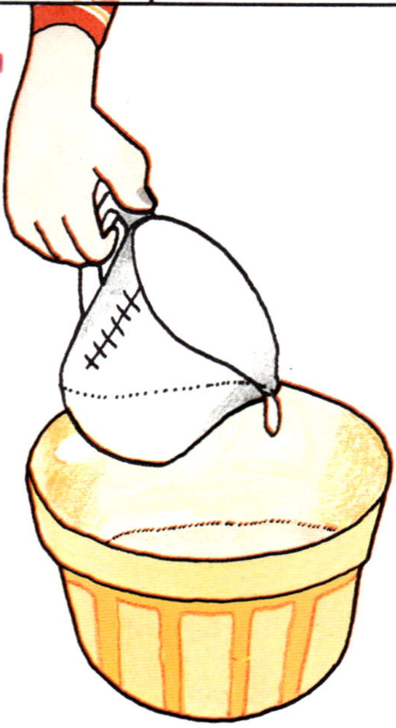

Add the water a little at a time and mix with your fingers until you have a thick dough.

5

If you have time, place your pastry dough in the refrigerator for 20 minutes before rolling out. This makes it stretchy and easier to use.

You can use this dough for the recipes on the next two pages.

Jam Tarts

Shortcrust pastry
(use recipe on page 28)
Jam
Rolling pin
Teaspoon
Cup or pastry cutter
Muffin tray

1

Roll out the pastry on a floured table top, turning it around until it is ¼ inch thick.

2

With a cutter or cup, cut out the tarts. Press each one into a greased muffin tray.

3

Put a teaspoon of jam into each tart. Do not overfill.

350°
Middle shelf
10 minutes

Hot Dog Roll-ups

Shortcrust pastry
(use recipe on page 28)
6 hot dogs
Water
Knife
Cookie sheet

1 Make shortcrust pastry as on page 28.

2 Cut the hot dogs into halves.

3 Roll out the pastry and cut it into four strips, each a little wider than the hot dog halves.

4 Cut each strip into three pieces.

5

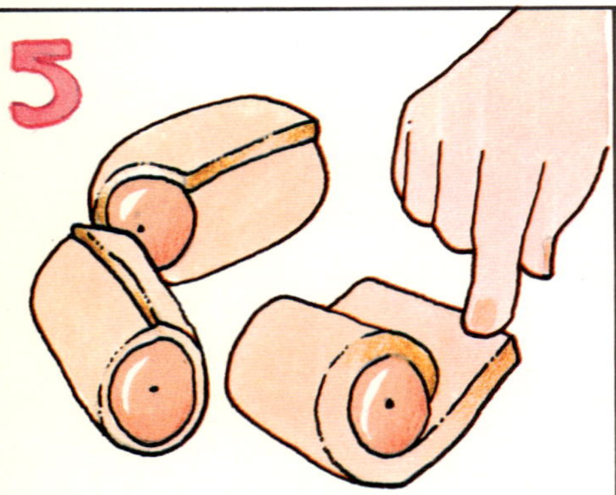

Roll a half of a hot dog into each piece of pastry. Wet the edge of the pastry with your finger to help it stick.

6 Put the rolls onto the cookie sheet and bake.

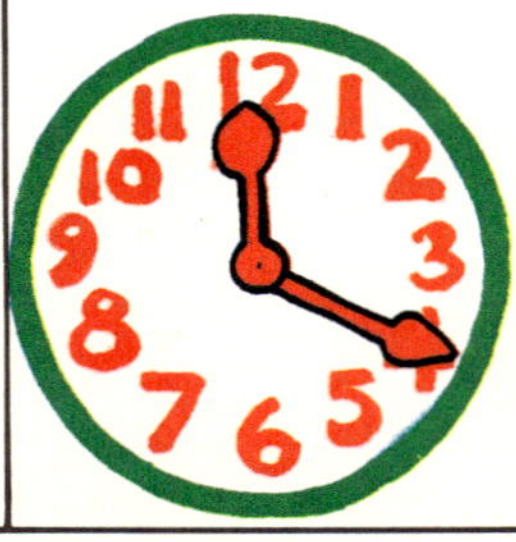

400°
Middle shelf
20 minutes

Cheese Straws

1 cup all-purpose flour
¼ cup butter or margarine
½ cup cheese
Pinch of salt
Pinch of pepper
Cold water
Teaspoon, grater
Bowl
Cookie sheet
Wire rack
Rolling pin
Dish, blunt knife

1

Grate the cheese into a dish.

2 Put the flour and butter into a bowl and mix with your fingers until it forms little crumbs.

3

Add the grated cheese, 4 teaspoons of water, and mix.

4 Continue to add water, a little at a time, until the dough sticks together but is not soggy.

5 Roll out the pastry on a floured tabletop until it is ½ inch thick.

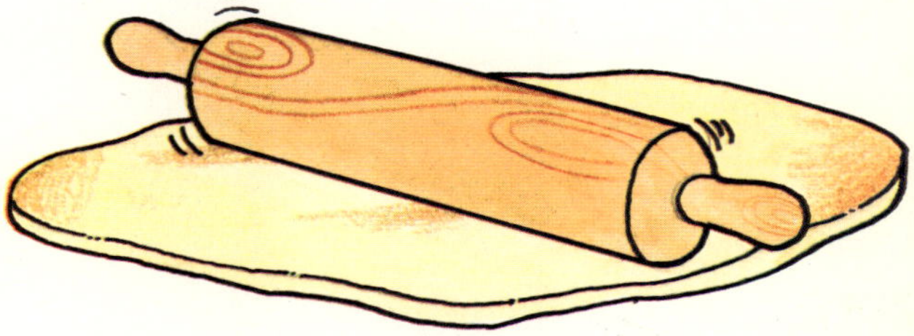

6 Cut the pastry into fingers, or any shapes you like, and put them on the greased cookie sheet to bake.

350°
Middle shelf
15 minutes

7 Allow the cheese straws to cool on a wire rack.

Hot Spicy Muffins

2 cups all-purpose flour
½ teaspoon mixed spice (cinnamon, nutmeg, ginger)
¼ cup shortening
2 tablespoons butter or margarine
2 tablespoons sugar
½ cup raisins
1 egg, 1 apple
Teaspoon, grater
Bowl, cup
Cookie sheet
Rolling pin, saucer

1 Peel, core, and grate the apple.

2

Put the flour and spice into the bowl, and rub in the shortening and butter.

3 Add the sugar and raisins.

4 Mix to a soft dough with the egg and apple.

5 Sprinkle a little flour onto a tabletop and roll out the dough, to a thickness of about ½ inch.

6 Using the cup, cut out circles and put them on the greased cookie sheet.

Iced Cupcakes

½ cup butter or margarine
½ cup sugar
2 eggs
1 cup all-purpose flour
⅔ cup confectioners' sugar
½ cup of water
Food colorings
Bowl
Wooden spoon
Paper cupcake holders
Baking pan
1 tablespoon baking powder

1 Mix butter and sugar to cream.

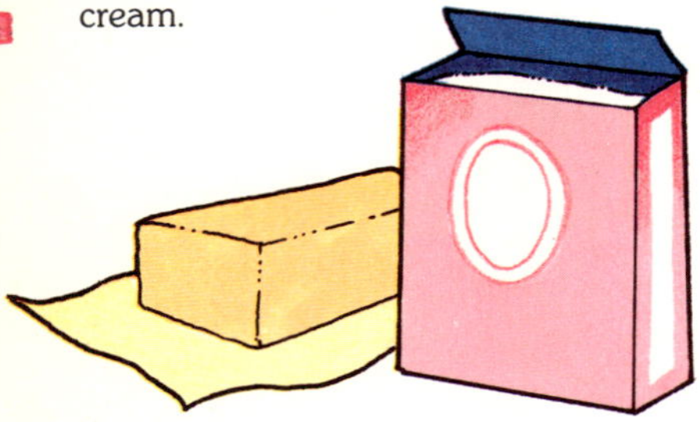

2 Add eggs one by one.

3

Add the flour and baking soda and mix well.

4

Place cupcake holders on baking pan. Fill each cup half way with mixture.

5

375°
Middle shelf
15 minutes

6

Mix confectioners' sugar and water, a little at a time, until thick, to make icing.

7

Divide icing into 3 cups and add different food colorings.

8 When cakes are cool, decorate with icing.

Gingerbread Snakes

¼ cup soft butter or margarine
4 tablespoons sugar
1 tablespoon molasses
1¼ cups all-purpose flour
1 tablespoon milk
1 tablespoon ground ginger
Bowl
Wooden spoon
Cookie sheet

1

Mix the butter and sugar.

2 Add the molasses and mix.

3

Add the all-purpose flour, ginger, and milk and mix well.

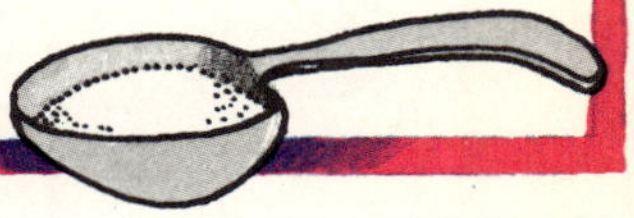

4

On a floured tabletop, shape the mixture into small balls.

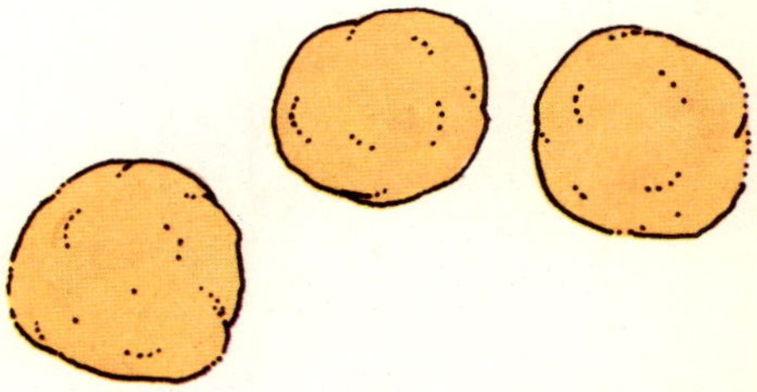

5 Shape the balls into lengths and then into snakes.

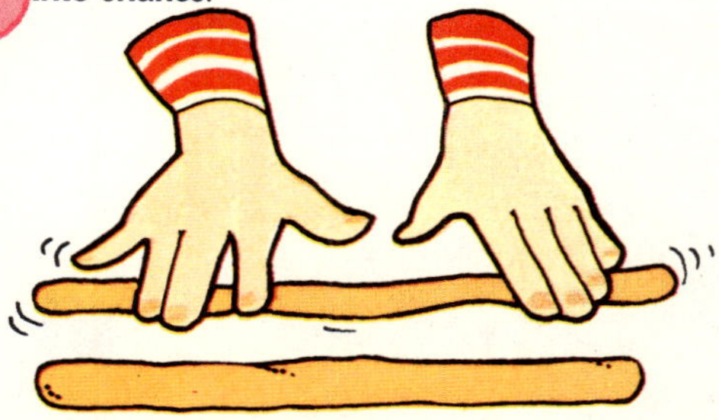

6 Place the snakes on a greased cookie sheet and bake.

7

350°
Top shelf
15 minutes

15 mins.

Apple Puffs

2 cooking apples
 or a can of apple sauce
6 teaspoons sugar
A little flour
1 packet defrosted puff pastry
Rolling pin
Baking pan
Cup of water
Blunt knife
Plate
Spatula

1

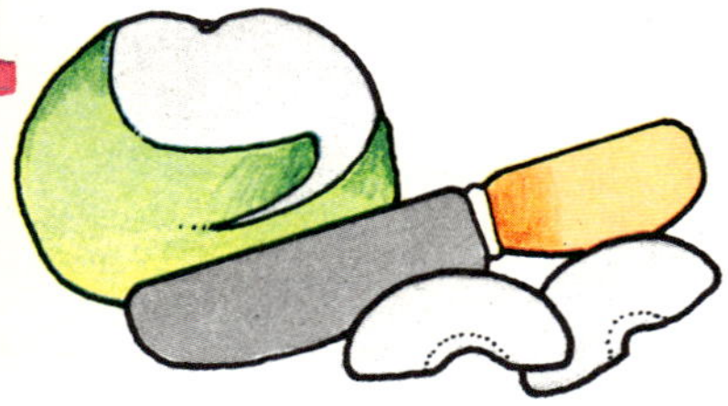

Peel, core, and slice the apples.

2

Flour the table and roll out the pastry until it is ¼ inch thick.

3

Cut the pastry into six squares.

4

Put a little apple and sugar on the center of each square.

5

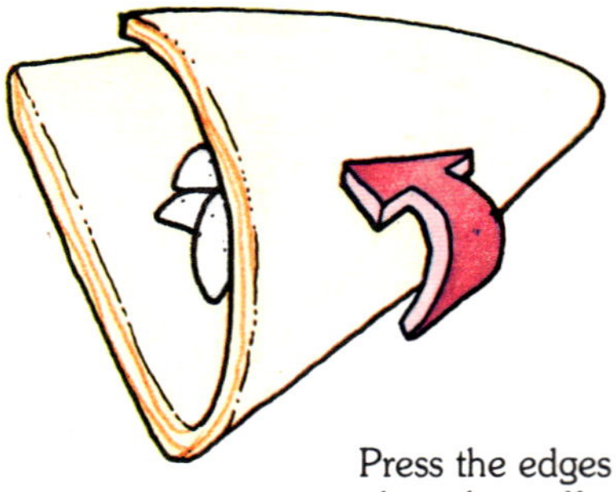

Wet the edges of each square and fold over the pastry to form an apple-filled triangle.

Press the edges carefully and place the puffs on the baking pan.

6

425°
Middle shelf
15-20 minutes

7

Remove puffs from the oven when the tops are brown and puffed up.

Chocolate Chip Cookies

¼ cup butter or margarine
4 tablespoons sugar
1 egg
Vanilla extract
¾ cup all-purpose flour
½ cup chocolate chips
Bowl, wooden spoon
Cup, tablespoon
Cookie sheet
Teaspoon
Wire rack
Spatula

1

Put the butter and sugar into a bowl and mix well.

2

Break the egg into a cup, add a few drops of vanilla extract, and mix.

3

Put the egg mixture into the bowl and mix well.

4

Add the flour and stir in with a tablespoon.

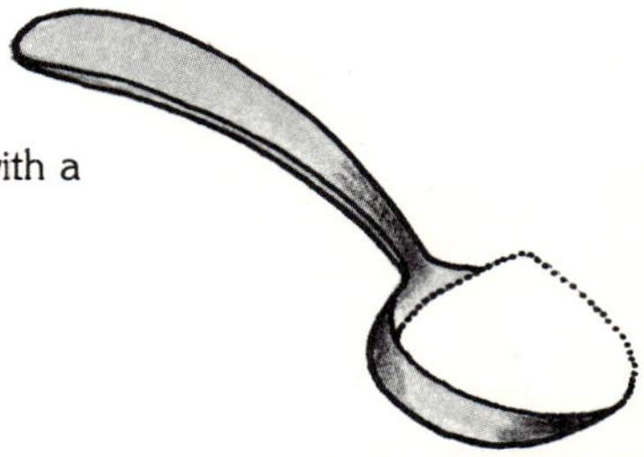

5

Add the chocolate chips to the mixture.

6 Using the teaspoon, drop the mixture onto a greased cookie sheet to form small round cookies.

350°
Middle shelf
10 minutes

10mins.

7 Allow to cool on a wire rack.

Banana Bread

1¾ cups all-purpose flour
¼ cup soft butter or margarine
1 egg
¼ cup sugar
grated rind of 1 lemon
3 ripe bananas
A little milk
Small dish, fork
Grater, bowl
Loaf pan
Wire rack

1 Mash the bananas in the small dish with the fork.

2 Put the flour into the bowl, add the butter, and rub it into the flour with your hands.

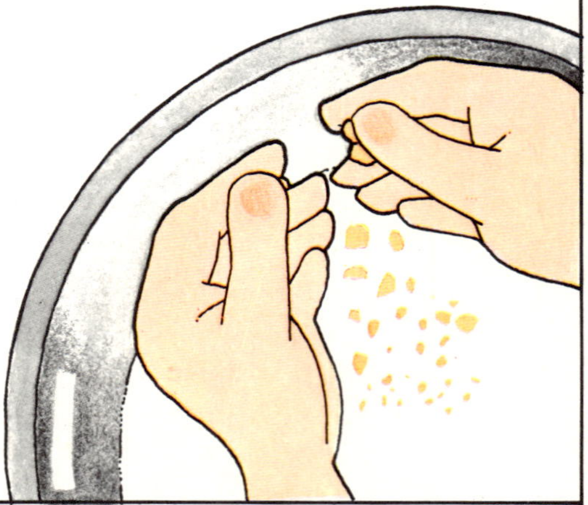

3 Now add the egg, mashed bananas, sugar, and lemon rind and mix thoroughly.

4 If the dough is crumbling, add a little milk to soften it, but do not make it too wet.

5

Grease and flour the loaf pan and spoon the dough into it.

6

When the bread is baked, let it cool for 5 minutes before turning it out onto a wire rack.

Brownies

1 cup all-purpose flour
¼ teaspoon baking soda
Pinch of salt
¼ cup shortening
½ cup sugar
2 tablespoons water
1 12-ounce package
chocolate chips
2 eggs
¼ cup chopped walnuts
Wax paper
Baking pan, 9″ × 11″
Saucepan
Wooden spoon

1 Put the shortening, sugar, and water into a saucepan. Stir them over a moderate heat until they are melted.

2 Take the saucepan off the stove and mix in the chocolate chips until they are melted.

3 Add the eggs, one at a time, and mix well.

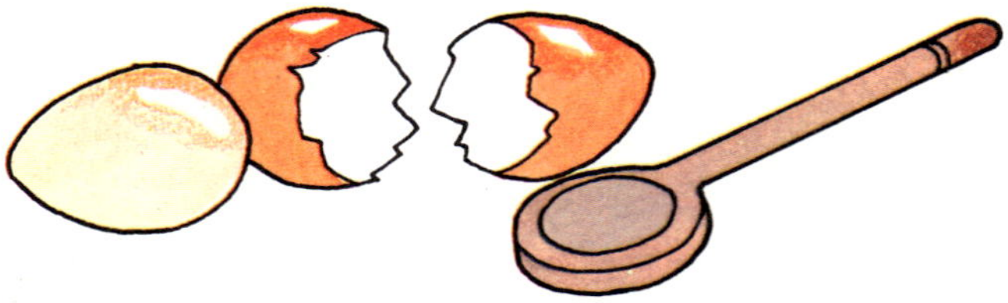

4 Add the flour, baking soda, and salt, and beat.

5 Add the chopped walnuts.

6

Line the pan with greased wax paper.

7

Pour in the mixture and bake.

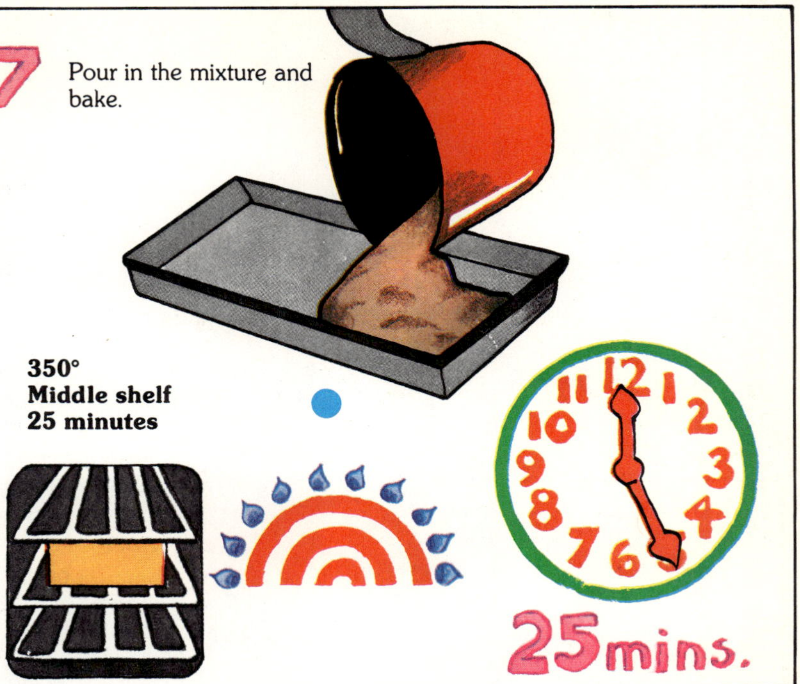

When the brownies are baked, let them cool and then cut them into about twelve pieces.

Raisin Cookies

½ cup butter or margarine
½ cup sugar
1¾ cups all-purpose flour
2 tablespoons mixed spice
(cinnamon, nutmeg, ginger)
1 cup raisins
1 egg
Bowl
Wooden spoon
Rolling pin
Blunt knife
2 cookie sheets
Spatula

1 Put the butter and sugar into the bowl and mix well.

2

Add the flour, mixed spice, fruit, and egg, and mix well.

3

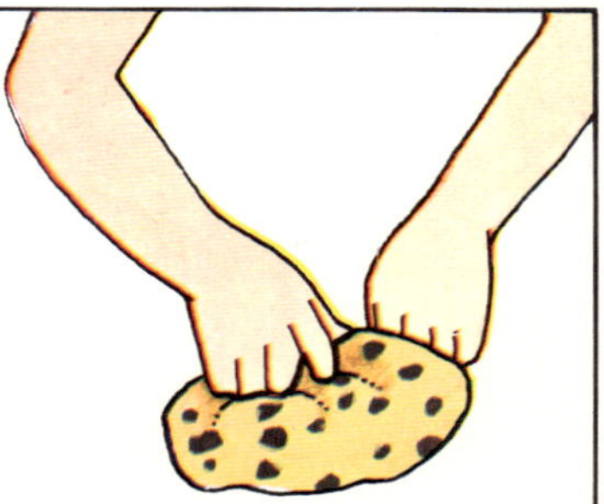

Put the mixture onto a floured tabletop and knead.

4 Roll out the dough to a thickness of ¼ inch.

5

Cut out shapes with a knife or cutter, using all the dough.

6

Put the cookies onto the cookie sheets.

350°
Top two shelves
15 minutes

Shortbread Wedges

- ⅓ cup soft butter or margarine
- 4 level tablespoons confectioners' sugar
- 1¼ cups all-purpose flour
- 2 tablespoons sugar
- Wire rack
- Bowl
- Wooden spoon
- Fork
- Round shallow cake pan
- Cooking oil
- Blunt knife

1 Put the butter and confectioners' sugar into the bowl and mix them with the spoon.

2

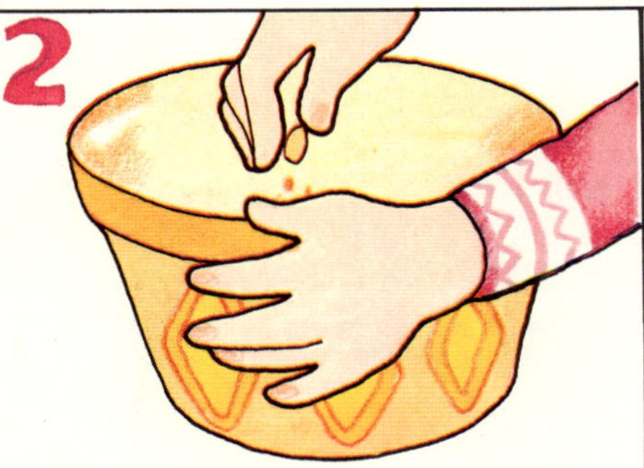

Add the flour and mix with your hands.

3

Grease the pan with oil.

4

Put the dough into the pan and press it down.

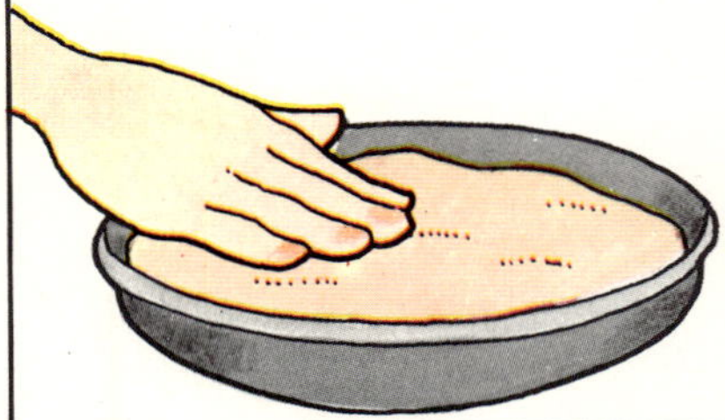

5 Prick the dough all over with the fork prongs, and divide it into eight sections with the blunt knife.

350°
Middle shelf
35 minutes

6

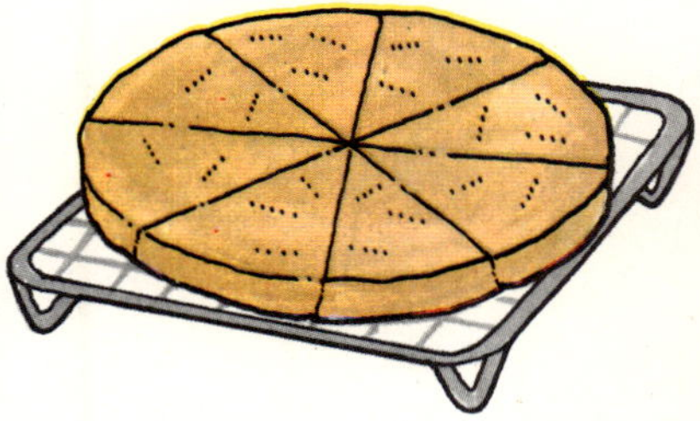

When the shortbread is baked, allow it to cool for 10 minutes, and turn it out onto a wire rack.

7

Turn the shortbread right side up and sprinkle it with sugar.

8

When cool, cut the wedges apart.

Making a Meal for Family and Friends

Menus

You can have a party for your friends with food you make yourself!

Here are three meals you can make for your family and friends using recipes from this book.

1. Cheese and pineapple spikes
   Grilled ham and cheese sandwiches
   Brownies

2. Cheese straws
   Salad sandwich boats
   Chocolate chip cookies

3. Milk shake
   Hot dog roll-ups
   Raisin cookies

Here is something for a morning or afternoon snack: a tea party for kids — featuring milk shakes for tea!

Cinnamon toast
Banana bread
Shortbread wedges
Milk shakes

Serving Food

Doing special things at the table can make a party out of ordinary food. Here are some ideas for making your meal a special event.

1. Put a flower in a napkin at each person's place.
2. Make place cards for each person at the table. On each card, put the person's name and a small drawing of something he or she likes.
3. Make paper placemats with pictures of things that remind you of each person at the table.
4. Cover the table with brown wrapping paper and let your guests decorate the tablecloth before you serve the food.
5. Make a centerpiece of stuffed animals. Give them nuts or other dry foods to hold. Or put food on small dishes for them.

Food Facts

Your body needs many different kinds of food to help you grow, stay healthy, and have the energy to do what you want to do. Here is a list of food elements and the foods that provide them.

Protein

Your body uses protein to build its muscles and bones. High protein foods include dried peas and beans; meat, fish, and poultry; lentils and nuts; and milk, cheese, and eggs.

Fats

Fats are a source of energy and vitamins. Cream, butter, vegetable oils, mayonnaise, and bacon are all high in fat.

Fiber

High fiber foods help your body digest other foods. They also promote healthy gums and teeth. Raw fruit, vegetables, and whole grain breads and cereals are high in fiber.

Vitamins

Vitamins are necessary to prevent certain diseases and sicknesses. They also help your body grow and develop well. Foods with high or special vitamin content include yeast, wheat germ, fruits and vegetables, cereal, liver, nuts, fish, milk, and eggs.

Minerals

Minerals are necessary for the growth and strength of teeth and bones. Leafy green vegetables, iodized salt, dried fruit, seafood, liver and other meat, and milk, cheese, and eggs are mineral sources.

To be sure that your body has all the fuel it needs, feed it well. Here is a plan for a well-fed day:

2 fruits (one citrus)
2 vegetables
3 cups of milk
2 servings of protein foods
4 servings of whole grain bread or cereal

More Books For Kid Cooks

Here are some more books about cooking. Look at the list. If you see any books you would like to read, see if your library or bookstore has them.

Beatrix Potter Country Cookery Book. Lane (Warne)
Bread Book. Meyer (Harcourt Brace Jovanovich)
Breads and Biscuits (First Cookbook Library). de Villiers/van der Berg (Gareth Stevens)
Chemistry and Cooking. Carona (Prentice-Hall)
Cookies, Cakes, and Candies (First Cookbook Library). de Villiers/van der Berg (Gareth Stevens)
Drinks and Desserts (First Cookbook Library). de Villiers/van der Berg (Gareth Stevens)
The Fairy Tale Cookbook. McClenahan (Prentice-Hall)
Getting Ready To Cook (First Cookbook Library). de Villiers/van der Berg (Gareth Stevens)
Kids Are Natural Cooks. Parents' Nursery School (Houghton Mifflin)
Kids' Kitchen Takeover. Stein (Workman)
The Little House Cookbook: Frontier Foods From Laura Ingalls Wilder's Classic Stories. Walker (Harper & Row)
Once Upon a Cook Book. Kaplan (Good Sign)
One Dish Meals (First Cookbook Library). de Villiers/van der Berg (Gareth Stevens)
Pooh Cook Book. Ellison (Dell)
Vegetables and Salads (First Cookbook Library). de Villiers/van der Berg (Gareth Stevens)
Walt Disney's Mickey Mouse Cookbook (Western)
What to Do When Your Mom or Dad Says . . . "Make Your Own Breakfast or Lunch." Berry (Living Skills)
Wonderful Wizard of Oz Cook Book. Bayley (Macmillan)

For Grown-ups

It's Fun to Cook! provides a simple and enjoyable way for you to introduce children to some of the basic principles of cooking — and to enjoy with them the delicious things you prepare together.

Keeping in mind that children won't eat what they don't like, we've created recipes that use some of children's favorite ingredients. In addition to the recipes, the sample menus and a discussion of "Food Facts" (pages 44-46) show children how to plan a meal that is balanced both aesthetically and nutritionally.

The combination of clear text, helpful and appealing illustrations, and added ideas for things to do make *It's Fun to Cook!* an enjoyable and instructive experience for children and grown-ups alike.